LIFE

Around the World

A LIFESTYLE COLORING BOOK

Illustrated by Sarah Brody

LIBERTY
STREET

Imagine the view of Manhattan from the windows
in Lady Liberty's crown. Watch the water glisten as you
glide in a gondola down a Venice canal.

Explore the enduring temples of Angkor Wat or the
man-made wonders of the Egyptian pyramids. Observe a herd
of zebras graze at the base of Mount Kilimanjaro.

Throughout the pages of this coloring book, you'll
find illustrations inspired by a collection of LIFE photographs.
Here we have selected 62 locations that will take you
on an adventure around the world.

Discover fascinating places and their historical and geographical
importance. Beautiful buildings, ancient ruins, and awe-inspiring
sculptures will make you want to plan your next adventure.

And remember, we travel not to escape life
but so life does not escape us.

AFRICA
A male lion dozes in the sunlight while
lounging in a cluster of rocks.

BEIJING, CHINA
This altazimuth at the Ancient Observatory was used to
determine the position of celestial bodies during the Ming
Dynasty and has wrought-iron dragon details.

PARIS, FRANCE
The decorative sculptures of the
Arc de Triomphe reflect the traditional architectural
style of the first half of the 19th century.

GRAND CANYON, ARIZONA
A view from above showcases the
Grand Canyon's stature. It averages 10 miles
across and is 277 miles long.

VENICE, ITALY
A man steers a gondola, a tapered 32-foot-long
flat-bottom boat, in a canal.

BEVERLY HILLS, CALIFORNIA
A street in Beverly Hills is lined with palm trees with
long plumes that sway in the breeze.

ASWAN GOVERNORATE, EGYPT
Statues of Rameses II at Abu Simbel temple are carved
from the sandstone cliff of the Nile's west bank.

LONDON, ENGLAND
The queen's messenger departs
Buckingham Palace with two briefcases carrying
dispatches for the Foreign Office.

PARIS, FRANCE
The Eiffel Tower is a 984-foot structure built of
open-lattice ironwork by Gustave Eiffel in 1889.

KENYA, AFRICA
A tower of giraffes, the tallest animals on earth,
congregate on Alexander Douglas Ranch.

COPENHAGEN, DENMARK
A bronze statue of Hans Christian Andersen's
Little Mermaid is perched on a rock in the harbor
along the Langelinie promenade.

WASHINGTON, D.C.
The U.S. Capitol's dome cost $1,047,291 to
construct in 1866 and is made with 8,909,200 pounds
of cast iron bound together.

ST. PETERSBURG, RUSSIA
Catherine the Great founded the
State Hermitage Museum in 1764, and it houses
over 3 million works of art.

LONDON, ENGLAND
The Tower Bridge was built in 1894 and spans
350 feet across the River Thames.

EGYPT

A felucca, a native riverboat with lateen sails, glides
along the Nile River, which stretches 4,132 miles.

NEW YORK, NEW YORK
Atop the Statue of Liberty, sightseers can take in the view from the windows in her crown.

SAMARKAND, UZBEKISTAN
Registan—"sandy place" in the local language—
was the central commercial plaza or bazaar in this city
on the Silk Road.

VERSAILLES, FRANCE
A Parisian couple stands in front of one of many intricate statues that decorate the Palace of Versailles.

PISA, ITALY
The Leaning Tower of Pisa slants about 4 degrees due to
the settling of its foundation during its construction.

HESSLER, GERMANY
A young man rides a horse-drawn cart through
a peasant village in the 1940s.

AGRA, INDIA
The Taj Mahal, built between 1631 and 1648,
is a marble mausoleum situated
on the south bank of the Yamuna River.

NORMANDY, FRANCE

A Gothic-style Benedictine abbey sits atop
Mont-St.-Michel, a rocky islet exposed to the
powerful tides of the English Channel.

ROME, ITALY
The Arch of Constantine features a composition of reused
materials from the Domitian, Trajan, and Hadrian periods.

IRELAND
A dog is perched on the back of a horse
pulling a jaunting cart.

ITALY

The *palazzi*, or villas, of Italy often feature well-manicured gardens and late-Renaissance architecture including detailed sculptures.

AFRICA

A leopard climbs a tree for a better vantage point
in search of prey or to take a nap.

VENICE, ITALY
Footbridges connect the buildings that line the canals,
the main thoroughfares in this city.

VATICAN CITY
From the gorgeous gardens of this villa,
there is a great view of the Michelangelo-designed
dome of St. Peter's Basilica.

KYOTO, JAPAN
The tiled roof and weathered wooden beams of this
temple are typical of historic buildings in Kyoto.

ROME, ITALY
A freestanding structure of stone and concrete,
the Colosseum seated some 50,000 spectators.

BOLÍVAR, VENEZUELA
Water cascades down Angel Falls, the
highest uninterrupted waterfall in the world
at nearly a kilometer high.

AFRICA

The African elephant is the world's largest land
mammal, with massive ears resembling the shape of
its home continent.

JAPAN

A geisha with painted lips and dressed in a traditional kimono stands beneath an open parasol.

SYRIA

Meharists, or members of a native Bedouin
camel cavalry commanded by French officers, travel
atop she-camel mounts.

KYOTO, JAPAN
Kiyomizu-dera Temple sits on Mt. Otowa, a peak in the
Higashiyama range, and dates back more than 1,200 years.

LONDON, ENGLAND

Big Ben, a clock tower on the northern end of the
Houses of Parliament, chimes on the hour.

KENYA, AFRICA
At the base of Mount Kilimanjaro, a herd of zebra grazes
in the plains of Amboseli National Reserve.

MOSCOW, RUSSIA
Ivan the Terrible commanded that St. Basil the Blessed
be built to commemorate his military victories.

NEW YORK, NEW YORK
The Chrysler Building, located on the East Side
of Manhattan, features an Art Deco–inspired steel spire
and was built in 1928.

ATHENS, GREECE
The Parthenon was built to shelter a monumental statue
of the goddess Athena sculpted from gold and ivory.

EASTER ISLAND, CHILE
These Moai statues, carved from
volcanic stone, are a sample of the 400 statues
across the Polynesian island.

ST. MORITZ, SWITZERLAND
The steeple of former French-Calvinist "Au Bois"
church peers above the frosty blanket of snow covering
the winter-resort village.

CAWDOR, SCOTLAND
In *Macbeth*, written in the spring of 1606,
Shakespeare drew inspiration from Cawdor Castle
for the place of Duncan's murder.

PRAGUE, CZECH REPUBLIC
Two men sit in rowboats at the base of a bridge
crossing over the Vltava.

TANZANIA, AFRICA
A parked car sits on the street in Zanzibar, an
African Island in the Indian Ocean.

ISTANBUL, TURKEY
The Hagia Sophia was built in about six years
during the Byzantine Empire, when Istanbul was
known as Constantinople.

MEXICO CITY, MEXICO
Cars pass by the Palace of Fine Arts in the densely
populated capital city of Mexico in the 1940s.

PRAGUE, CZECH REPUBLIC
The capital of the Czech Republic, Prague is known for its colorful baroque buildings and Gothic churches.

EDINBURGH, SCOTLAND
Edinburgh Castle, a historical fortress
and active military base, dominates the skyline
of Scotland's capital.

BRUGES, BELGIUM
Winding canals, cobbled streets, and the medieval towers
of the Church of Notre Dame steeple and the
market square belfry distinguish the city of Bruges.

ST. MORITZ, SWITZERLAND
A woman enjoys a ride on a sleigh drawn by horses
with festive bells in 1947.

LONDON, ENGLAND
In 1837, Queen Victoria was the first sovereign
to live at Buckingham Palace, located
in Westminster.

MACHU PICCHU, PERU
The ancient ruins of Machu Picchu are
renowned for their sophisticated dry-stone walls
fused together without any mortar.

BEIJING, CHINA
A stone lion statue guards the south entrance
of the Forbidden City.

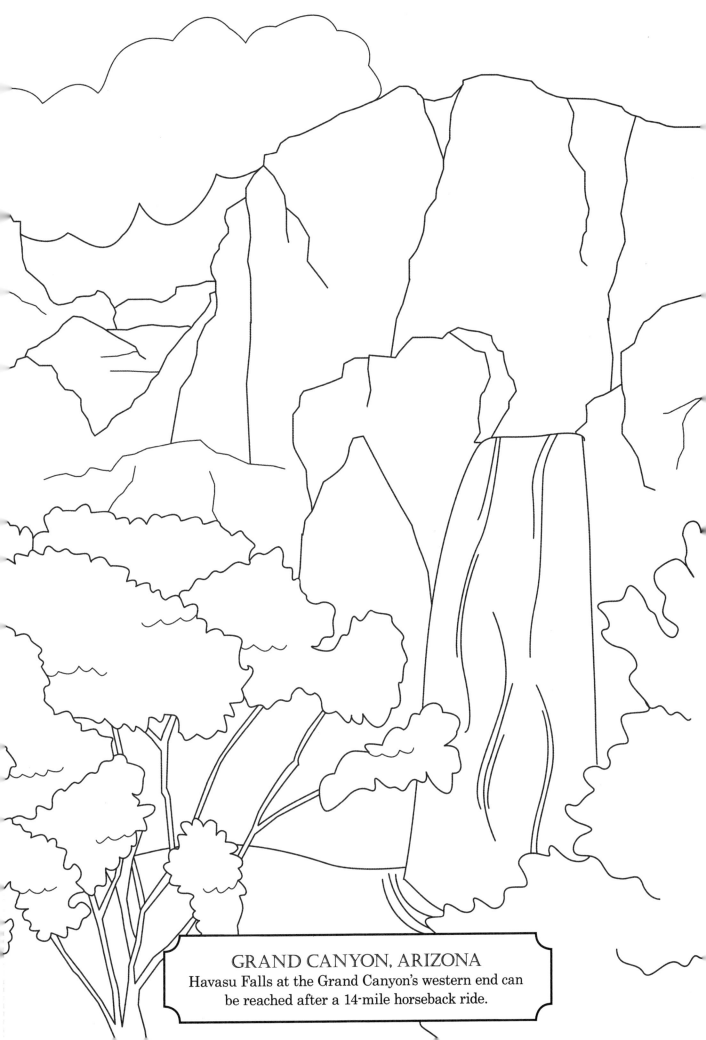

GRAND CANYON, ARIZONA
Havasu Falls at the Grand Canyon's western end can
be reached after a 14-mile horseback ride.

PETEN, GUATEMALA
Tikal, the largest excavated site on the
North American continent, features archaeological
remains of the Mayan civilization.

GIZA GOVERNORATE, EGYPT
Built when Egypt was a rich and powerful
civilization, the Great Sphinx and Pyramids are
man-made wonders.

YUCATAN, MEXICO
The Mayans built Chichen Itza in the 6th century and dedicated it to their godlike leader, Kukulcan.

WYOMING
A herd of wild horses stampedes across a river
in the wilderness of Wyoming.

SALISBURY PLAIN, ENGLAND
Neolithic builders constructed Stonehenge
with roughly 100 massive sandstone slabs. It took
an estimated 1,500 years to complete.

FLORIDA KEYS
A boat docked at the pier sways in the gentle waves
of the South Florida waters.

KRONG SIEM REAP, CAMBODIA
The Angkor Wat temple ruins feature
unique architecture of the ancient civilization
of the Khmer Empire.

Published by Liberty Street, an imprint of Time Inc. Books
225 Liberty Street
New York, NY 10281

LIBERTY STREET and LIFE BOOKS are trademarks of Time Inc.

Interior illustrations by Sarah Brody
Cover and interior design by Georgia Morrissey
Cover illustration by Jan Gerardi
Director of Photography: Christina Lieberman
Picture Editor: Rachel Hatch
Project Manager: Hillary Leary
Copy Chiefs: Rina Bander, Parlan McGaw
Editoral Assistant: Nicole Fisher

ISBN 10: 1-68330-752-6
ISBN 13: 978-1-68330-752-5

First edition, 2016

1 QGS 16

10 9 8 7 6 5 4 3 2 1

Time Inc. Books products may be purchased for business or promotional use. For
information on bulk purchases, please contact Christi Crowley in the Special Sales
Department at (845) 895-9858.

To order Time Inc. Books Collector's Editions, please call (800) 327-6388, Monday
through Friday, 7 a.m.–9 p.m., Central Time.

We welcome your comments and suggestions about Time Inc. Books.
Please write to us at:
Time Inc. Books
Attention: Book Editors
P.O. Box 62310
Tampa, FL 33662-2310

timeincbooks.com

Illustration created from a photograph by Eliot Elisofon/LIFE/The Picture Collection